Author:
Mark Bergin was born in Hastings, England. He has illustrated an award winning series and written over twenty books. He has done many book designs, layouts and storyboards in many styles including cartoon for numerous books, posters and adverts. He lives in Bexhill-on-sea with his wife and children.

Editorial Assistant:
Rob Walker

Published in Great Britain in MMXII by Scribblers, a division of Book House
25 Marlborough Place, Brighton BN1 1UB

ISBN: 978-1-908177-70-4

S A L A R I Y A

1 3 5 7 9 8 6 4 2

A CIP catalogue record for this book is available from the British Library.

Printed and bound in China.

PAPER FROM
SUSTAINABLE
FORESTS

Visit our website at
www.book-house.co.uk
or go to **www.salariya.com** for **free** electronic versions of:
You Wouldn't Want to be an Egyptian Mummy!
You Wouldn't Want to be a Roman Gladiator!
You Wouldn't Want to be a Polar Explorer!
You Wouldn't Want to sail on a 19th-Century Whaling Ship!

Previous editions © MMXI

It's fun to draw Safari Animals
ISBN-13: 978-1-906714-33-8

It's fun to draw Princesses and Ballerinas
ISBN-13: 978-1-907184-69-7

It's fun to draw Dinosaurs and other prehistoric creatures
ISBN-13: 978-1-906714-34-5

ART IDEAS

The beginner's fun book of art skills

Mark Bergin

Contents

How to use this book

Get started!

Start by following the numbered splats on the left hand page.

Step by step!

These simple steps will ask you to add some lines to your drawing. The new lines are always drawn in red so you can see how the drawing builds from step to step.

splat-a-facts!

Learn some fantastic splat-a-facts about what you are drawing!

Tyrannosaurus rex

Tie-RAN-oh-sore-us

1 Draw a rectangle with a half circle.

2 Draw a smaller rectangle and another half circle.

3 Draw dots for a nose and an eye, add zig-zag lines for teeth.

4 Add lines for the body.

5 Draw in the arms and the legs.

you can do it!

Paint the Tyrannosaurus green then draw lines with a yellow wax crayon, then colour in with felt-tip or paint. The wax crayon acts as a resist to the paint.

splat-a-fact

Tyrannosaurus rex means 'tyrant lizard king'. A large meat eater, Tyrannosaurus ate large dinosaurs like Triceratops.

68

Read the 'You can do it!' splats to learn about drawing and shading techniques you can use.

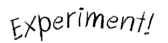

Experiment!

Find out what happens when you draw with a wax crayon then colour over it with watercolour paint.

Mix colours!

Learn how to layer coloured crayons to make different colours. Create fantastic effects with watercolour paint.

Be inspired!

These pages are designed to build your confidence and creative skills. Each spread includes a finished, coloured drawing you can use as inspiration. Let your imagination go wild and see what amazing pictures you can create.

Try smudging pastels or sponging paint. Create a paper collage out of coloured paper.

69

Art materials

Felt-tip pens usually come in sets of many different colours. Fineliners make even thinner lines than felt-tip pens.

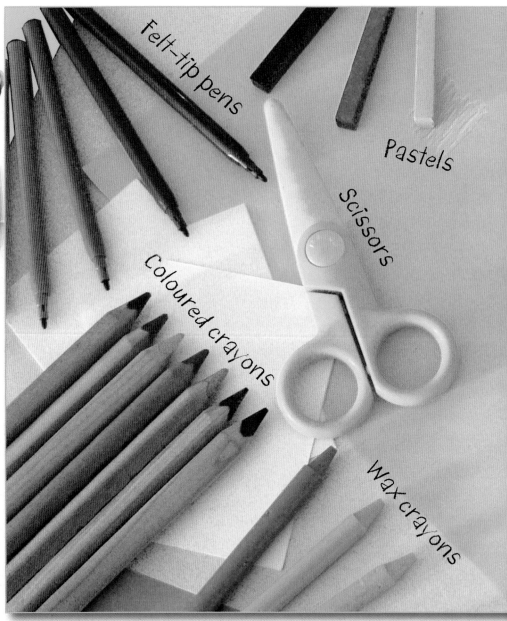

Felt-tip pens

Pastels

Scissors

Coloured crayons

Wax crayons

What you will need

The drawings and paintings in this book use materials which are easy to find in any shop that sells art equipment.

Paper

Cartridge paper is good for using with crayons, pastels and felt-tip pens.

Watercolour paper is thicker and the best paper to use watercolour paint on.

Try other paper, such as tissue paper, coloured paper and brown wrapping paper. Different coloured paper will change the colours you use on it.

crayons

Coloured crayons come in sets of different colours.

Wax crayons also come in sets, and can be used as a resist when using watercolours or coloured inks.

Pastels

Chalk pastels are easy to smudge and usually come in sets.

Chalk pencils are softer than coloured crayons, and they can be smudged.

Collage

For collage you will need scraps of coloured paper, glue and scissors. BE SURE TO GET AN ADULT TO HELP YOU WHENEVER YOU USE SCISSORS.

Brushes

You will need a fairly large paint brush for painting with watercolours and inks.

When painting you will also need a plastic container for water, and an old white plate for mixing paint. You may also need a small sponge.

Keeping clean

Before you start, put on an old apron or T-shirt. Protect the area you are working on with sheets of old newspaper. Have a rag and some paper towels ready, too. You can use these to wipe your brushes and to mop up spills.

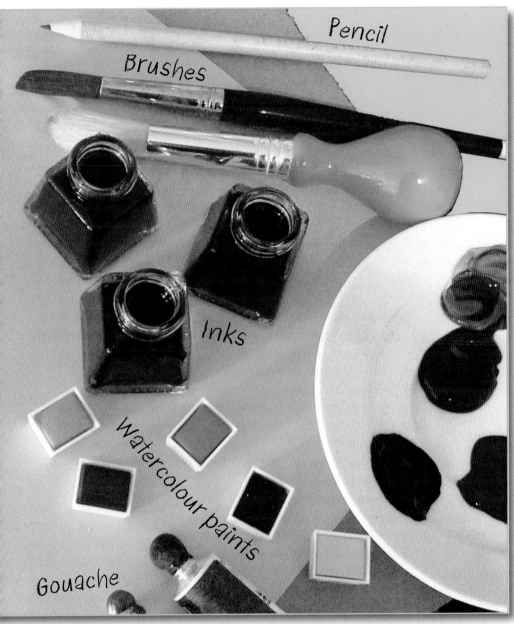

Pencil

Brushes

Inks

Watercolour paints

Gouache

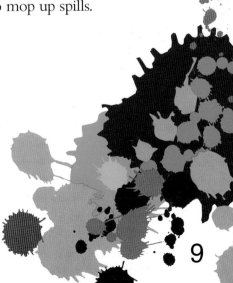

Paints

Watercolour and gouache are the paints used in this book, but you could try other types instead.

Inks

Inks come in small bottles and are very brightly coloured.

9

Zebra

1 Start with the head and a dot for the eye.

2 Add ears, mouth, nostrils and hair.

3 Draw in the neck to a bean-shaped body.

you can do it!
Use wax crayons for background texture painted over with watercolour paint. Use black felt-tip for the zebra's stripes.

4 Add the mane and the tail.

splat-a-fact
No two zebra stripes are exactly the same.

5 Draw four legs and hooves.

Lion

you can do it!

Use wax crayons to colour and a felt-tip for the lines.

1 Start with the head and add two dots for the eyes.

2 Add the nose, mouth and whiskers and draw in the mane.

splat-a-fact

Lions rest for about 20 hours each day.

3 Add the body with a curly tail and four legs with big paws.

12

13

Giraffe

1 Start with the head, mouth, hair and dots for the eyes and nostrils.

2 Draw two long lines for the neck and an oval shape for the body.

3 Add a mane, two ears and tufts on the horns.

you can do it!

Use wax crayons for texture, painted over with water colour paint. Use brown ink for the giraffe pattern and a felt-tip for the lines.

Splat-a-fact
Giraffes are the tallest animals on earth.

4 Draw in four legs and a tail.

15

Ostrich

1 Start with the head, adding a beak and a dot for the eye.

2 Draw two lines for the neck.

3

Draw an oval shape with a flat bottom for the body. Add a line at the front and the wing.

4 Add two legs with clawed feet and big tail feathers.

you can do it!

Use oil pastels, and use your finger to smudge them. Use a felt-tip for the lines.

16

17

Eagle

Start with the head and the body.

Add an eye, a beak, two feet and tail feathers.

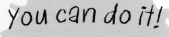

Draw two wings.

you can do it!

Use wax crayons for the feather shapes and textures. Paint over with watercolour paint. Use a felt-tip for the lines.

Splat-a-fact

Eagles have excellent eyesight and razor-sharp talons.

4 Add the wing feathers.

Wildebeest

1 Start with the head and the horns.

2 Add two ears and dots for the eyes and nostrils.

splat – a fact
A wildebeest is also called a gnu (noo).

you can do it!
Add colour with watercolour paint and use a sponge to dab more colour on for added texture. Use a felt-tip for the lines.

3 Draw the body shape and neck.

4 Add four legs and a tail.

Elephant

1 Start by cutting out the shape of the head.

2 Cut out the tusk and add a dot for an eye.

3 Cut an oval for the body.

4 Cut out the tip of the tail, four legs and draw in the toenails.

22

Leopard

you can do it!
Use coloured pencils and
felt-tip for the lines.
Use both for the
leopard's spots.

1 Start with the head.

2 Add ears, nose, mouth
and a dot for an eye.

3 Draw in the
neck and the body.

4 Add whiskers
and a tail.

Splat-a-fact

Leopards are great
climbers and like to
eat and sleep in trees.

5 Draw in four legs
and paws.

24

Warthog

1 Start with the head and a dot for the eye.

2 Draw in neck, hair, tusks and ears.

Splat-a-fact

A warthog kneels on its front legs to eat.

3 Draw the body shape.

You can do it!

Use a dark pencil for the outline and add colour with watercolour paint.

4 Add four legs, a tail and two dots for nostrils.

27

Thomson's gazelle

1 Start with the head and add a dot for the eye.

2 Draw two horns, ears, a nose and the cheek marking.

3 Add the neck.

4 Draw an oval shaped body, a tail and body markings.

you can do it!
Use coloured pastel pencils and smudge the colours with your finger. Draw the outline with felt-tip.

Splat-a-fact
A Thompson's gazelle has excellent sight, hearing and sense of smell.

5 Add the tail and black-tipped four legs.

Crocodile

1 Start with the head.

2 Add a nostril, eye, teeth and two small bumps.

3 Draw two lines for the body and tail and a line for its belly.

you can do it!
Use coloured inks and a felt-tip for the lines.

4 Add four legs, spikes on its back, lines across its belly and above the eye.

30

Baboon

Splat-a-fact

A group of baboons is called a troop.

1 Start with the head and chest.

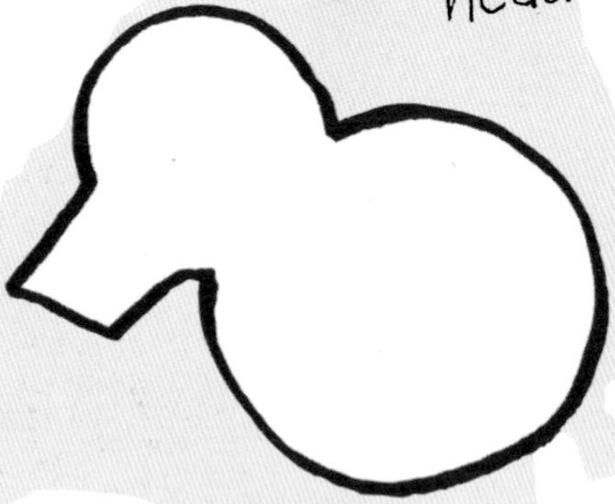

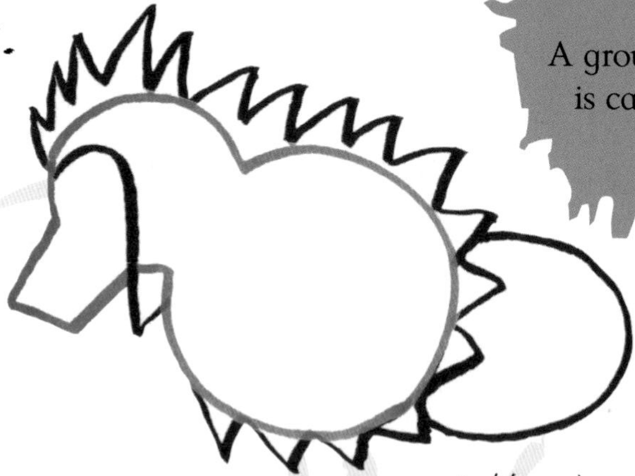

2 Add the body and lots of fur.

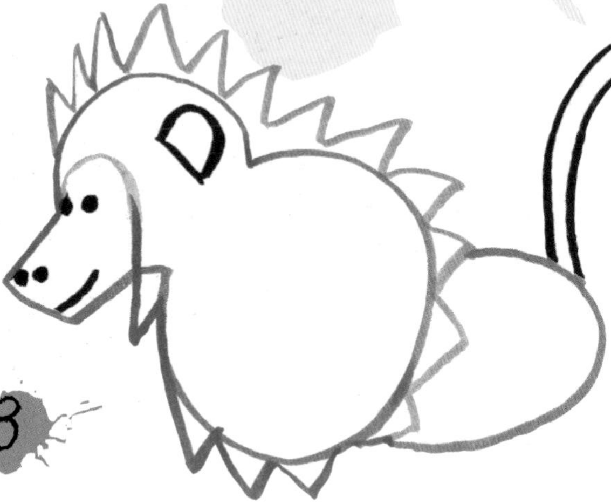

3 Draw in the tail, one ear and dots for eyes and nostrils.

4 Add two front legs and two back legs.

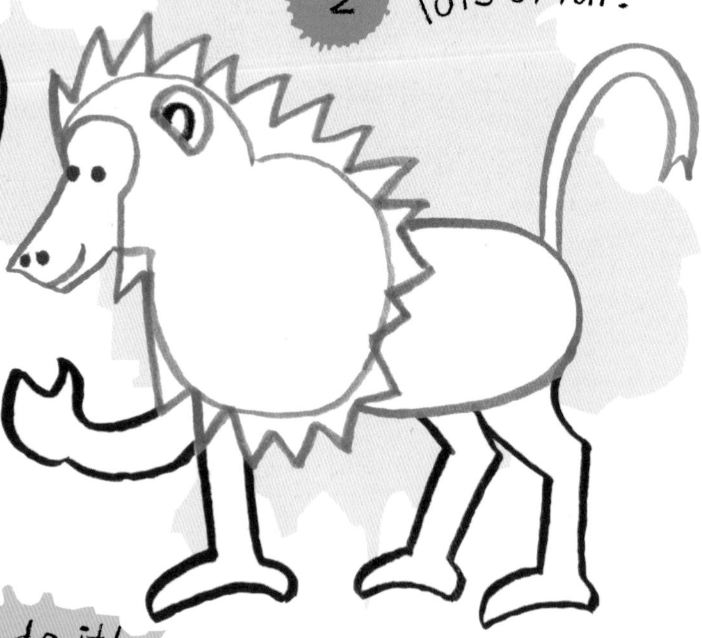

You can do it!

Use wax crayons for texture and paint over it with watercolour paint. Use felt-tip for the lines.

Hippo

1 Start with the head
and two dots for
the eyes.

2 Add two ears and
a mouth.

3 Draw a big
oval body.

4 Add a tail and four
legs with toenails.

splat-a-fact
Hippos spend most of
the day in water but
they do not swim.

Cheetah

1 Start with a head.

2 Add a dot for the eye and the mouth.

3 Add a long oval shape for the body, two lines for the neck and a dot for the nose.

you can do it!

Draw the outlines in brown felt tip. Colour in with coloured pencils.

4 Add the tail.

5 Add four legs.

splat-a-fact

A cheetah can run as fast as a car - up to 75 miles per hour!

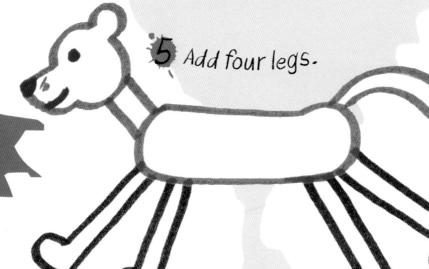

36

Princess Anna

1 Start with the head. Add nose, mouth and dots for eyes.

2 Add the arms and the top.

3 Draw in the hair and crown.

Splat-a-fact!
Princesses often live in castles.

you can do it!
Use a felt-tip for the lines and add colour using coloured pencils. Use the pencils in a scribbly way to add interest.

3 Add the dress and the feet.

38

Louise

1 Start with the head. Add a nose, mouth and dots for eyes.

2 Add the hair and an ear.

you can do it!
Use a brown felt-tip for the lines and add colour using pencils.

3 Draw in the dress.

splat-a-fact!
Ballerinas have to work hard and practise every day.

4 Add the arms and legs.

5 Add dress details and a bow.

Henrietta

 1

Start with the head. Add a nose, mouth and dots for eyes.

 2 Add the hair.

3

Draw in the tutu top and a big circle for the skirt.

you can do it!

Use wax crayons for all textures and paint over with watercolour paint. Use a blue felt-tip for the lines.

4

Add the legs.

5 Draw the arms.

Splat-a-fact!

Ballerinas can wear out 2 to 3 pair of points in one week.

42

Princess Margot

1 Start with the head. Add the nose, mouth and dots for the eyes.

you can do it!
Use wax crayons for all textures and paint over using coloured inks. Sponge some of the inks for added interest.

2 Add the dress.

3 Draw in the arms and the feet.

4 Add the crown and the hair.

5 Draw in the details of the dress.

splat-a-fact!

Once upon a time a princess befriended a frog. Then the frog turned into a handsome prince!

45

Princess Lisa

1 Start with the head. Add a nose, mouth and dots for eyes.

2 Add hair and a crown.

3 Draw in the top.

splat-a-fact!

Princesses have a different dress for each day of the year.

4 Add the arms and a handbag.

you can do it!

Use wax crayons for all textures and paint over with watercolours. Sponge some of the inks for added interest.

5 Draw the dress and feet.

46

Marina

1 Cut out the head and stick down. Draw on a mouth and a dot for the eye.

2 Cut out the tutu top and stick down. Cut out the skirt shape and stick down.

you can do it!

Start with a piece of coloured paper for the background. Cut out shapes for the spotlight and floor. Stick them down. Now cut out all the shapes for the ballerina and stick them down in the order shown.

3 Cut out the legs and feet. Stick the legs down first then add shoes.

4 Cut out the hair and stick down. Cut out the arms and stick down.

MAKE SURE YOU GET AN ADULT TO HELP YOU WHEN USING SCISSORS!

48

splat-a-fact!
A tutu can take about
60-70 hours to make.

49

Princess Helena

 1 Start with the head. Add a mouth and a dot for the eye.

2  Add the hair and crown.

3  Draw in three circles for the top.

Splat-a-fact!
Princesses appear in lots of fairy tales.

4  Add the arms.

You can do it!
Use wax crayons for the colour and a blue felt-tip for the lines.

5 Draw the dress and feet.

Princess Melissa

1 Start with the head. Add a nose, mouth and dots for eyes.

2 Draw in the dress.

3 Add the arms.

splat-a-fact!
Princesses don't usually do their own washing.

you can do it!
Use a soft pencil for the lines and add colour using watercolour paint.

4 Draw in the ropes and the swing. Add the feet.

5 Add the hair and crown.

Jennifer

 1 Start with a head. Add a nose, mouth and dots for eyes.

 **2** Add the hair.

 **3** Draw in the dress.

you can do it!
Add colour using coloured pencils. Use a black felt-tip for the lines, the shoes and the pattern on the tutu.

 **4** Add the arms and legs.

5 Shade in the dress and shoes.

splat-a-fact!
Ballerinas need to have strong ankles and knees.

Princess Nicole

1 Start with the head. Add a nose, mouth and lines for eyes.

you can do it!
USe a felt-tip for the lines and add colour using coloured pencils. Use the pencils in a scribbly way to add interest.

2 Draw in the top of the dress.

3 Add the rest of the dress.

splat-a-fact!
Princesses need lots of mattresses.

4 Add the arms and feet.

5 Draw in the hair and crown.

Princess Heather

1 Start with the head. Add a nose, mouth and dots for eyes.

2 Add the hair.

3 Add the hat and veil.

you can do it!

Use a green felt-tip for the lines and add colour using watercolour paint.

splat-a-fact!

A princess has everything she wants - beautiful dresses, handbags, tiaras and jewels.

5 Add the skirt and the feet.

4 Draw in the arms and sleeves.

Amanda

1 Start with the head. Add a nose, mouth and dots for eyes.

2 Add the hair and ears.

3 Draw in the tutu.

you can do it!

Use a purple felt-tip for the lines and add colour using coloured inks.

4 Add the arms and legs.

splat-a-fact!

Dancing 'en pointe' is performed by standing on the tips of your toes.

5 Finish off the details on the tutu.

Kirsten

1 Start with the head. Add nose, mouth and dots for eyes.

2 Add the hair.

3 Draw in the tutu.

you can do it!

Use a purple felt-tip for the lines and add colour with soft, chalky pastels. Smudge and blend some of the colours to add interest.

4 Add the arms and legs.

Splat-a-fact!

'Pas de deux' means a dance for two.

5 Finish off the details of the dress. Add a hairband.

Fiona

1 Start with the head. Add a mouth, nose and a dot for the eye.

 **2** Add the hair.

 **3** Draw in the tutu.

you can do it!

Use wax crayons to add colour and a blue felt-tip for the lines. Smudge or blend the colour for more interest.

4 Add the legs.

5 Draw in the arms.

Splat-a-fact!

It can take over 100 yards of tulle to make a tutu.

Diplodocus

Di-plod-OH-kuss

1 Start with the head.

2 Add a dot for the eye and two leaves.

3 Draw two lines for the neck.

4 Draw an oval shape for the body.

5 Draw four legs.

6 Draw two long lines for a tail.

you can do it!
Use felt-tip for the lines and colour in with crayon, using your fingers to smudge colours together.

splat-a-fact
Diplodocus had the longest tail of any animal that has ever walked on earth.

splat-a-fact
Fifteen tall men lying end to end in a line would measure the same length as a Diplodocus.

Tyrannosaurus rex

Tie-RAN-oh-sore-us

1 Draw a rectangle with a half circle.

2 Draw a smaller rectangle and another half circle.

3 Draw dots for a nose and an eye, add zig-zag lines for teeth.

4 Add lines for the body.

5 Draw in the arms and the legs.

you can do it!

Paint the Tyrannosaurus green then draw lines with a yellow wax crayon, then colour in with felt-tip or paint. The wax crayon acts as a resist to the paint.

Splat-a-fact

Tyrannosaurus rex means 'tyrant lizard king'. A large meat eater, Tyrannosaurus ate large dinosaurs like Triceratops.

Ankylosaurus

An-keel-oh-SAW-rus

1 Start with the head and eyes.

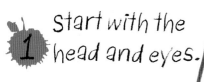

2 Add a mouth, a nostril and three spikes.

3 Draw a big oval shape for the body.

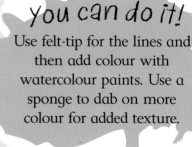

you can do it!

Use felt-tip for the lines and then add colour with watercolour paints. Use a sponge to dab on more colour for added texture.

4 Draw two lines for the tail, with small ovals at the end.

splat-a-fact

The Ankylosaurus could swing its big, bony tail to club its enemies.

5 Draw four legs.

6 Draw a line through the middle of the body.

7 Add spikes.

Pteranodon

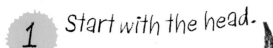

Terr-AN-oh-don

1 Start with the head.

2 Add a tongue and a dot for the eye.

3 Draw two lines for the neck and a circle for the body.

4 Draw in the curved shape of the wings.

splat-a-fact

A Pteranodon's wings, made of leathery skin, were as large as a hang glider.

5 Add the legs and the feet.

you can do it!

Use a soft 4B pencil for the lines and add colour with watercolour paint.

Dimetrodon

Dye-MET-ra-don

1 Start with the head.

2 Add the mouth, a nostril and a circle with a dot for the eye.

5 Draw a big curved shape with straight lines in it.

3 Draw two lines for the neck, joined to a big oval.

4 Draw two lines to add the tail.

Splat-a-fact
A Dimetrodon's back 'sail' was made of tough skin and long bones.

6 Add four legs.

Parasaurolophus

Para-saw-ROLL-oh-fuss

1 Start with the head with a small mouth and a dot for the eye.

2 Draw two lines for a crest and add nostrils.

3 Draw two lines for the neck, an oval shape for the body and two curved lines for the tail.

you can do it!
Paint the Parasaurolophus yellow and pink then scribble lines with a yellow wax crayon. Add colour with paint. The wax acts as a resist to the paint.

splat-a-fact
Parasaurolophus had the biggest head crest of all the duck-billed dinosaurs.

4 Draw in two legs and two arms.

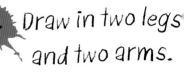

76

Pachycephalosaurus

pack-ee-seff-ah-low-saw-rus

1 Start with a head and an eye.

2 Add the mouth, a nostril, two nose spikes and some small circles.

3 Add two lines for the neck, a big oval, two curved lines for the tail and two arms.

Splat- a fact

A Pachycephalosaurus was the same height as a double decker bus when it stood upright to feed.

you can do it!

Use a felt-tip for the lines and add colour with chalky pastels. Use your finger to smudge the colours.

4 Add two legs with clawed feet.

stegosaurus
stegg-oh-SAW-rus

1 Start with the head.

2 Add the mouth and dots for the nostrils and eye.

3 Draw two lines for the neck and a circle for the body.

4 Draw two lines for the tail and add four legs.

You can do it!
Use felt-tips for the lines and add colour with wax crayons. Use different kinds of scribbly crayon marks to add variety.

5 Add kite-shaped plates on its back and spikes at the end of the tail.

Splat-a-fact
Some of the Stegosaurus's back plates were about 2 ft tall (61 cm) and 2 ft (61 cm) wide.

Iguanodon

Ig-WAN-oh-don

1 Start with the head.

2 Add the mouth and dots for the eye and nostril.

3 Draw lines for the neck and an oval shape for the body.

4 Draw two lines for the tail.

5 Add two legs, two feet and two arms.

splat-a-fact

The Iguanadon was first found in England.

you can do it!

Use felt-tip for the lines and add colour with watercolour paints. Make a smudged effect by adding green paint to the yellow while it is still wet.

Liopleurodon

Lee-oh-PLOOR-oh-don

1 Cut out the shape of the head.

2 Draw in the eye, nostril and zig-zag mouth.

you can do it!

Cut out the shapes from coloured paper with wax crayon stripes. Stick these on to a sheet of blue paper. Use felt-tip for the lines and white gouache for the air bubbles.

2 Cut out an oval shape for the body and a pointed tail.

3 Cut out four pointed flippers.

MAKE SURE YOU GET AN ADULT TO HELP YOU WHEN USING SCISSORS!

Splat-a-fact
Liopleurodon had strong flippers to speed through water after its prey.

4 Glue all of the body into place and add the head last to overlap.

84

styracosaurus

Sty-RACK-o-saw-rus

1 Start with the head: add spikes, a horn, an eye and a mouth.

2 Draw a circle for the body.

Splat-a-fact
Styracosaurus means 'spiked lizard'.

3 Draw two curved lines for the tail.

you can do it!
Use felt-tip for the lines and colour in with oil pastels. Smudge colours together with your finger.

4 Add four legs.

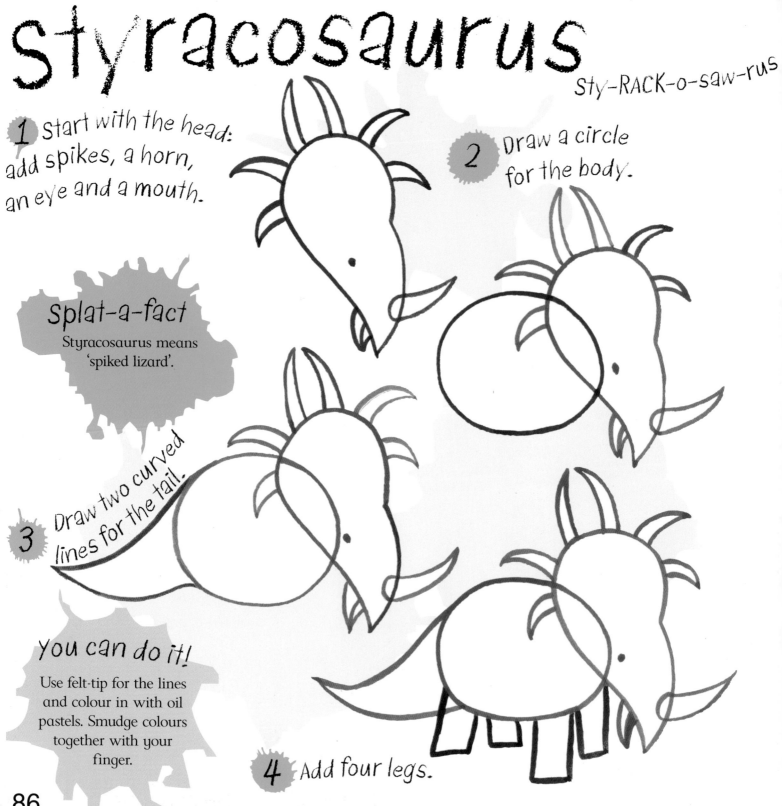

Velociraptor

Veh-LOSS-er-rap-tor

1 Start with the head and a dot for the eye.

2 Add nostril, mouth and teeth.

3 Draw in two lines for the neck and an oval shape for the body.

4 Draw two lines for the tail and two arms.

you can do it!
Use felt-tip for the lines and add colour usng coloured pencils.

splat-a-fact
Velociraptors starred in the film *Jurassic Park*.

5 Add two legs with clawed feet.

Triceratops

Try-SERRA-tops

1 Start with the head and a dot for the eye.

2 Draw in horns and the mouth.

you can do it!

Use a felt-tip pen for the lines. Add colour with watercolour or ink. Use wax crayon then paint on top, the wax will act as a resist. Make a smudge on the Triceratops by adding orange paint to the pink paint while it is still wet.

3 Draw in an oval shape for the body.

splat-a-fact

A Triceratops was almost twice the length of a rhinoceros.

4 Add four legs and draw two curved lines for the tail.

90

Corythosaurus

core-ith-o-SAW-russ

2 Add a nostril, the mouth, and an egg-shaped bump on top.

3 Draw two lines for the neck joined to a large oval shape.

1 Start with the head and add a dot for the eye.

you can do it!

Use a felt-tip pen for the lines and add colour with watercolour paint.
Use purple ink on the yellow body while the paint is still wet.

Draw two curved lines for the tail.

4

splat-a-fact

Corythosaurus had a bony crest on top of its head.

5 Add a curved line to the body and draw two arms and two legs.

92

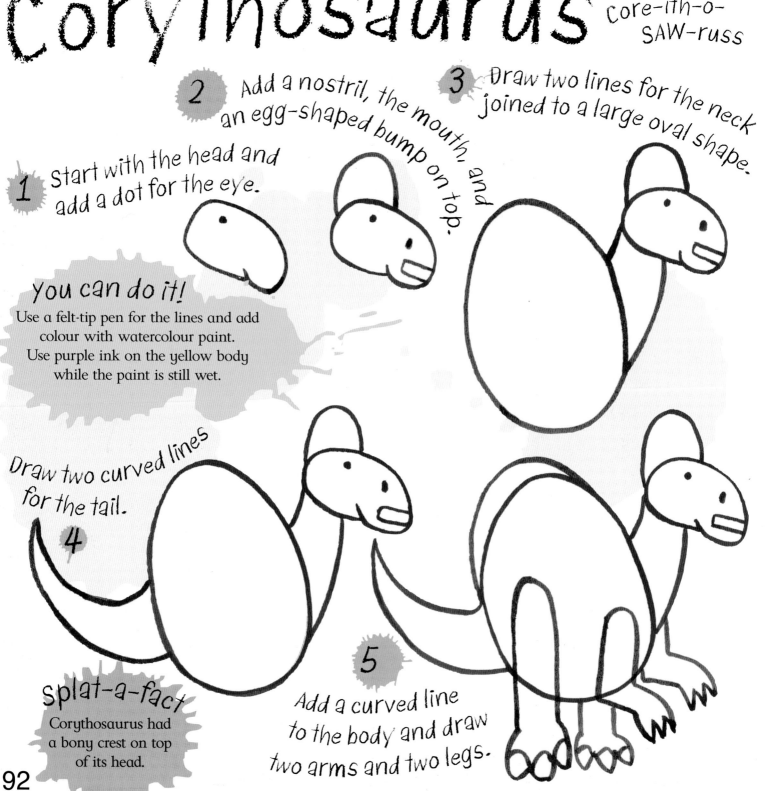

93

Glossary

Background   The area or scene behind the main object.

Befriend   To make friends with someone.

Crest   A lump that sticks out, usually on the head of a bird or animal.

Crosshatching   A type of shading that uses two or more sets of parallel lines to make dark areas.

Gouache   Paint that can be used thickly or mixed with water like watercolour.

Handsome   Good-looking.

Hooves   The hard covering on the tips of the toes of some animals.

Mane   The long hair along the top and sides of the necks of some animals.

Outline   The line or lines that show the shape of something.

Paper collage   A picture that uses pieces of shaped paper, stuck down to make a design.

Pastel   A soft, crumbly stick for drawing with.

Paws   An animal's feet with claws or nails.

Points (ballerina's)   A ballerina's pointed shoes.

Razor sharp   Extremely sharp.

Resist, resistant   A substance used to stop watercolour or ink from colouring.

Shading   The lines or marks used to show areas of light and dark on a picture.

Smudge, smudging   The use of a finger to blur or soften pastel or crayon marks.

Soft pencil   Pencils can be hard or soft. A 4B pencil is soft and makes thick, black marks.

Sponging   The use of a sponge to put paint onto areas.

Talons   Claws.

Technique   A clever way of doing something to create a desired effect.

Texture   How the object is drawn to look hard, soft, rough or smooth.

Tiara   Like a crown, often with jewels.

Tulle   Fine net fabric.

Tusk   A long pointed tooth.

Tutu   A short, full skirt worn by ballerinas.

Veil   A length of netting attached to a lady's hat.

Watercolour   Paint that can be mixed with water. The more water that is added, the paler the colour it makes.

Index